#presidents
FOLLOW THE LEADERS

Scholastic Inc.

29 photos

310 followers

90,026 following

Author: JOHN OWEN

Los Angeles

Library of Congress Cataloging-in-Publication Data available

ISBN 978-0-545-85127-5

10 9 8 7 6 5 4 3 2 1   15 16 17 18 19

Printed in the U.S.A. 40
First edition, September 2015
Book design by Jessica Meltzer

#presidents
FOLLOW THE LEADERS

13 photos

5.4M followers

6 following

Virginia

Username: GENERALWASHINGTON1776
Name: George Washington
1st President
Born: 1732, Westmoreland County, Virginia
Years in Office: 1789–1797 (two terms)
Vice President: John Adams (@IndependenceAdams)
Spouse: Martha Washington
Bio: #First! And one of the greatest, #TBQH. As #general, I won us #independence in the #AmericanRevolution. As #prez and #FoundingFather, I set the example for those who came next.

⭐ **76 LOVES**

🖊 #Firstpresident . . . so, since I'm #numberone, it's only right that I have just #onetooth left! #pearlywhite #justbeingme 😀

 BAMIMOBAMA That's not good! You gotta brush! #Cmon #dentalhygiene!!

 GENERALWASHINGTON1776 Why, if I'd spent all my time trying to keep my teeth from falling out, I'd hardly have had time left to win the Revolution! #keytosuccess

 BAMIMOBAMA It takes, like, two seconds! 🙁 Children, don't listen to this man!!! At least about brushing!!!

1776 photos

300K followers

14 following

Mass.

Username: INDEPENDENCEADAMS
Name: John Adams
2nd President
Born: 1735, Braintree, Massachusetts
Years in Office: 1797–1801 (one term)
Vice President: Thomas Jefferson (@DeclarationsOfJeff)
Spouse: Abigail Adams
Bio: #Revolutionaryhero. Lover of #stronggovernment. #Fulldisclosure, I can be a little #grouchy . . . lol. #DadOfAPrez, shout-out to my son @TheQuotableQuincy.

⭐ **130 LOVES**

🖊️ #TBT: Things were rather exciting back in those early days of the #AmericanRevolution! For example, the #BostonTeaParty was this huge rager where British tea was tossed overboard! It made the ocean taste very #delicious for several days.

 AYOUNGBOSTONLAD I don't think you're supposed to drink seawater, President Adams! 😨

 INDEPENDENCEADAMS Of course not. But, you see, they put the tea in the water, so the water turned to tea.

 AYOUNGBOSTONLAD I really, REALLY don't think that's how it worked.

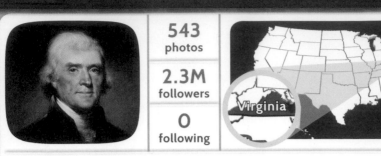

543 photos
2.3M followers
0 following

Virginia

Username: DECLARATIONSOFJEFF
Name: Thomas Jefferson
3rd President
Born: 1743, Shadwell, Virginia
Years in Office: 1801–1809 (two terms)
Vice President: Aaron Burr (@DARINGAARON_BDAWG);
George Clinton
Spouse: Martha Jefferson
Bio: Author of the #DeclarationOfIndependence, the most important document in American history. #SorryConstitution. #Piratefighter. Expanded America big-time with the #LouisianaPurchase and sent #LewisAndClark to explore it.

⭐ **44 LOVES**

✒ #TGIF! Y'all may know me as one of the most famous presidents, but there's more to me than that! In my spare time, I like to design #amazinghouses (like Monticello, the one I live in), invent #newgadgets (like the #swivelchair), even translate new versions of #TheBible. Also love #Farming #Science #Philosophy #LearningAncientLanguages #StartingColleges.

 THE_HONESTABE1860 Man. Is there anything you don't like doing?

 DECLARATIONSOFJEFF I DO dislike getting out of my pajamas. In fact, I often do all my work in them! #WhoNeedsPants #PJs4lyfe 😬

72
photos

107K
followers

0
following

New Jersey

Username: DARINGAARON_BDAWG
Name: Aaron Burr
3ʳᵈ Vice President
Born: 1765, Newark, New Jersey
Years in Office: 1801–1805 (one term)
President: Thomas Jefferson (@DeclarationsOfJeff)
Bio: #ambitious #cunning #controversial – Founding Fathers don't get any cooler than me, folks.

⭐ **51 LOVES**

Who says VPs are boring? When I was veep, I shot and killed fellow Founding Father @AlexanderHamilton because I thought he had insulted me! #LoveDuels #DuelLife #DuelAllDay #BestVPEver

 GENERALWASHINGTON1776 That's not better than being boring! That's worse! He helped create our entire economy! And you weren't even convicted of murder for that! 😢

 DARINGAARON_BDAWG If you don't like that, how about how I later started plotting to take over the Louisiana Territory and make a new country? And how then I got charged with treason but got off from that, too?

333 photos

230K followers

18 following

Virginia

Username: LILJCONSTITUTION
Name: James Madison
4th President
Born: 1751, Port Conway, Virginia
Years in Office: 1809–1817 (two terms)
Vice President: George Clinton; Elbridge Gerry
Spouse: Dolley Madison
Bio: #FatherOfTheConstitution and one of the authors of the #BillOfRights – still the foundation of the #USGovernment! Battled the British in the #AmericanRevolution AND the #WarOf1812. And if you must know: Yes, I'm the #smallestprez. #fivefootfour #100pounds #sizedoesntmatter #stayhumble

⭐ **122 LOVES**

Ah . . . nothing like a #blazingfire. #Cozycentral. OH MY GOSH 😨 THAT'S NOT A COZY FIRE THAT'S @THEWHITEHOUSE! THE BRITISH ARE BURNING IT!

 DOLLEYMADISON Relax! I thought quickly and rescued many #preciousartifacts – including the official portrait of @GeneralWashington1776!

 LILJCONSTITUTION Oh, bless you, my dear! And you also got all my #powderedwigs, I hope?

 DOLLEYMADISON Uh, no, There were way too many to carry.

 LILJCONSTITUTION This is a dark day.

52
photos

140K
followers

10
following

Virginia

Username: JIM_USA_FLAG_GUY_USA
Name: James Monroe
5th President
Born: 1758, Westmoreland County, Virginia
Years in Office: 1817–1825 (two terms)
Vice President: Daniel D. Tompkins
Spouse: Elizabeth Monroe
Bio: Last prez who was a #FoundingFather. Gosh, it feels nice to be in office when most people in the country support me! #EraOfGoodFeelings

⭐ **80 LOVES**

∽ Okay, people. I didn't want it to come to this, but I'm #SICKandTIRED of @Europe always getting into OUR biz. You need to, like, leave us alone for once! #Srsly. If you come barging in on us #onemoretime . . .

 EUROPE What? What'll you do, Jamesy-boy?

 JIM_USA_FLAG_GUY_USA I'll make sure that in a few hundred years, when our movies are awesome, you won't be able to see anything! Not even on #Netflix! So keep out!

 EUROPE I'm sorry, we'll do whatever you say #anything

12 photos
129K followers
30 following

Mass.

Username: THEQUOTABLEQUINCY
Name: John Quincy Adams
6ᵗʰ President
Born: 1767, Braintree, Massachusetts
Years in Office: 1825–1829 (one term)
Vice President: John C. Calhoun
Spouse: Louisa Adams
Bio: I see you, Dad! #SonOfAPrez. Like @IndependenceAdams, I'm not exactly the warmest guy . . . and I only served #OneTerm. After that, it's back to the #HouseOfRepresentatives, where I worked hard for decades to #fightslavery!

⭐ **5 LOVES**

✒ Ah . . . now that I'm in @TheWhiteHouse I can do what I've always dreamed of . . . #skinnydipping in the #icecold Potomac River every morning.

 INDEPENDENCEADAMS Hey there, son . . . #congrats . . . but do you think that now that you're president . . . you should maybe quit it with the dips? #fatherknowsbest

 THEQUOTABLEQUINCY Hi, Dad! I can't hear you over this rushing river! Wow! This feels so good!

 INDEPENDENCEADAMS #facepalm

82
photos

4.7M
followers

202
following

South Carolina

Username: OLDHICKORY
Name: Andrew Jackson
7th President
Born: 1767, Lancaster County, South Carolina
Years in Office: 1829–1837 (two terms)
Vice President: John C. Calhoun; Martin Van Buren (@TheOriginalOK)
Spouse: Rachel Jackson
Bio: #ManOfThePeople! I extended the vote to more men than ever before! In my spare time, I simply love to #WinDuels. In fact, I've still got a bullet lodged in my chest from one of my victories! How many other presidents can say THAT?

★ **600 LOVES**

✎ Party at my place! #EveryonesInvited #StartedFromTheBottom #PioneerPresident #FamousGeneral #SoIDoWhatIWant

 THEWHITEHOUSE Surely you . . . you don't mean #EVERYONE, do you?

 OLDHICKORY Oh, def not. Just the entire general public In Washington, DC. Having giant parties every week. Say, are your floors #horseproof?

 THEWHITEHOUSE 😨

189 photos
12K followers
1 following

New York

Username: THEORIGINALOK
Name: Martin Van Buren
8th President
Born: 1782, Kinderhook, New York
Years in Office: 1837–1841 (one term)
Vice President: Richard M. Johnson
Spouse: Hannah Van Buren
Bio: #Bestbuds with @OldHickory – you da man, AJ! I helped invent the #DemocraticParty. But then the #PanicOf1837 financial crisis came along and started a #depression. #Gah. I've got a pretty big legacy outside all that: The phrase #OK is based on my nickname #OldKinderhook!

⭐ **1 LOVE**

〰️ #ShoutOut to my mentor, @OldHickory, who helped me win the presidency . . . and, more important, gave me the #confidence to rock these #sicksideburns. #SideburnsSwag #LongMayTheyWave 😀

 OLDHICKORY More than welcome, bro! All I ask in return is that you let me use them for #targetpractice sometimes. Gotta stay sharp for my #duels, y'know.

 THEORIGINALUK What? #noway! 😨

 OLDHICKORY I'll just take that as a yes. 😀

30 photos		
30 followers		Virginia
30 following		

Username: ILLWILL_H
Name: William Henry Harrison
9th President
Born: 1773, Charles City County, Virginia
Years in Office: 1841 (one term, one month in office)
Vice President: John Tyler (@TotallyTheActualPrez)
Spouse: Anna Harrison
Bio: Lookit – #famousgeneral. I'm a super-strong army general. I was in tons of battles. Nothing can get to me! #strongestprez
Hmmm what's going on? My nose feels a little sniffly. #achoo

⭐ **90 LOVES**

Perfect . . . caught a cold at my inauguration 😣 #Died31DaysLater #ShortestPresidency

 ILLWILL_H Hey, @TheWhiteHouse: Sorta #awkward, but you don't happen to need any #ghosts, do you?

 THEWHITEHOUSE Listen. We'd love to have you stay on in #ghostform, but you've been here such a short time we don't think you'd know your way around enough to haunt well.

 ILLWILL_H #fiddlesticks! 😣

27 photos

18K followers

0 following

Virginia

Username: TOTALLYTHEACTUALPREZ
Name: John Tyler
10th President
Born: 1790, Charles City County, Virginia
Years in Office: 1841–1845 (one term)
Vice President: None
Spouse: Letitia Tyler (1813–1842); Julia Tyler (1844–1862)
Bio: Yeah, I was #viceprez . . . until a cold struck, so now I'm #prez myself. @FillardMillmore, @TheTennesseeTailor, @ChetsFashionChest, @BuckingBroncoTeddyBear, @SilentCal, @GoGetEmHarry & @LBJAllTheWay – all VPs who became the prez in the same way. #StillPresident #StillHaveToListenToMe

⭐ **59 LOVES**

🖊 WOOHOO! Got the #WhiteHouseAllToMyself! This calls for a #celebrationdance #BOOYAH! #FirstVPToTakeOver!

 TOTALLYTHEACTUALPREZ Oh and #RIP to my dear friend and mentor @IllWill_H . . . sooooooo sad . . . #tear #crystagram #LikeISaidSooooooSad

 SENATORHENRYCLAY Would you consider holding a new election since the #Constitution doesn't yet make it clear who becomes president now? (And it won't till the #25thAmendment in 1967!)

 TOTALLYTHEACTUALPREZ I'll think about it! #QuicklyShutsDoor #InYourFace #SmellYaLater

47
photos

200K
followers

47
following

Username: VERYIMPORTANTVPs
Name: Vice Presidents
Bio: Yeah, we may not be as #highprofile as the #prez. We may not really have any #officialduties or #responsibilities. But still we're #veeps and we're #OnFleek. #WhateverThatMeans

William A. Wheeler

WILLIAM RUFUS DE VANE KING

NELSON A. ROCKEFELLER

SCHUYLER COLFAX

JOE BIDEN

⭐ **51 LOVES**

✒️ Pretty #steamed today. Check out this quote from first VP @IndependenceAdams: "My country has in its wisdom contrived for me the most insignificant office that ever the invention of man contrived or his imagination conceived." Other #veeps, what do you think about that? Sound off in the comments!

 ELBRIDGEGERRY_VP Wow! Talk about #disrespect! If @IndependenceAdams hates being #VP so much, why not just leave it and go be some president or something! 😠

 INDEPENDENCEADAMS I did become president.

48 photos

1.2M followers

40 following

North Carolina

Username: POLKADOTZ11
Name: James K. Polk
11th President
Born: 1795, Pineville, North Carolina
Years in Office: 1845–1849 (one term)
Vice President: George Mifflin Dallas
Spouse: Sarah Polk
Bio: Nobody knew who the heck I was when I was nominated for president. #Darkhorse. But they sure knew me after! I got the United States #madterritory in the #MexicanAmericanWar. Run for a #secondterm? Why? I accomplished everything I wanted to in one. #bossmove #ballerstatus #dropthemic

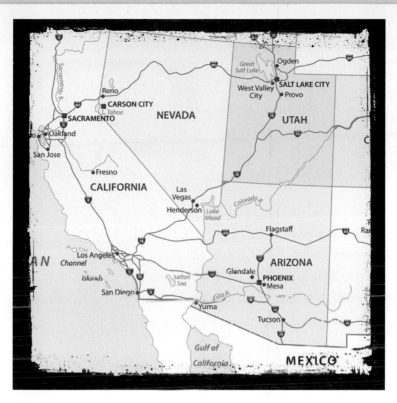

⭐ **37 LOVES**

✍️ YES. Just got TONS of new land for the United States. Now we stretch all the way across the continent, #FromSealToShiningSeal, just like that song! 😀

 CLINSTAGRAM Are you talking about "America the Beautiful"? The line is "from sea to shining sea."

 POLKADOTZ11 No! Like, you know, the different kinds of seals you can find on both coasts. All #shiny from the water.

 CLINSTAGRAM No, no. It's talking about the Atlantic and Pacific Oceans. Yours doesn't rhyme!

 POLKADOTZ11 Agree to disagree?

5 photos
1,330 followers
21 following

Virginia

Username: ROUGHNREADY_ZT
Name: Zachary Taylor
12th President
Born: 1784, Barboursville, Virginia
Years in Office: 1849–1850 (one term, 16 months in office)
Vice President: Millard Fillmore (@FillardMillmore)
Spouse: Margaret Taylor
Bio: Got the nickname #OldRoughAndReady as a #general in all kinds of wars. When I was elected, #slavery was finally becoming a big issue, and I came into office ready to work hard to #stopitsspread and keep the states together. But then I sorta . . . #piggedout and #diedinoffice. #Whoops

Margaret Taylor

VP

⭐ **771 LOVES**

🎵 It's #hothothot out! So cool down with one of my favorite ways to #beattheheat: eating a #MASSIVE bowl of cherries. Washed down with #TONS of #deliciousicedmilk!

 FILLARDMILLMORE #Pardonme, but that sounds sort of . . . #weird? #Icedmilk? #Huh?

 ROUGHNREADY_ZT Trust me! It's to die for. Literally! A year into my presidency, I ate all this stuff on a #blazinghot day and got #extremelysick and died from a weird stomach thing. But this stuff is so good I don't regret a thing!

71 photos
4,500 followers
4,500 following

New York

Username: FILLARDMILLMORE
Name: Millard Fillmore
13ᵗʰ President
Born: 1800, Moravia, New York
Years in Office: 1850–1853 (one term)
Vice President: None
Spouse: Abigail Fillmore
Bio: I was #bornpoor, but with #hardwork and #goodluck I became #rich . . . not to mention the vice president. And after @RoughNReady_ZT died, I became president, too! But, ah . . . yeah, my luck ran out a little then, and some of the policies I supported helped trigger the #CivilWar #whooooooops

⭐ **2,000 LOVES**

📝 #DomoArigato! My administration has opened relations with Japan! A wonderful opportunity for both nations. AND I FINALLY HAVE A SAMURAI SWORD! #HIYA! 🙂

 WHITEHOUSEBUTLER Mr. President! Stop! Stop swinging that around! Please!

 FILLARDMILLMORE You're right, you're right. I got carried away. It was wrong to #HIYΛΛΛΛ!!!!!!

 FILLARDMILLMORE Gosh. Why do all my employees keep unfollowing me? 😟

109 photos
880 followers
43 following

New Hampshire

Username: HANDSOMEPANTSPIERCE
Name: Franklin Pierce
14th President
Born: 1804, Hillsborough, New Hampshire
Years in Office: 1853–1857 (one term)
Vice President: William Rufus de Vane King
Spouse: Jane Pierce
Bio: #Supercute. #Totallydreamy. And like @FillardMillmore, I couldn't help but #stirthingsup and incite the Civil War. So, um, can we focus on those first two things?

⭐ **251 LOVES**

Some historians say I'm the most #handsome prez ever! Like this post if you #agree . . . and comment if you #alsoagree! #pickme #mcm #mancrushmonday

 KENNEDAYALLDAY Greetings, President Pierce! Thought you'd be interested to know, these days many historians think I'm the most handsome! #carryingthetorch #newgeneration

 HANDSOMEPANTSPIERCE Thank you for commenting, President Kennedy! Glad to know that, like many, you #alsoagree!

4 photos	
9 followers	
12 following	Penn.

Username: FOREVERALONE56

Name: James Buchanan

15th President

Born: 1791, Cove Gap, Pennsylvania

Years in Office: 1857–1861 (one term)

Vice President: John C. Breckinridge

Spouse: 🙁

Bio: Only president who never married. The #SouthernStates start leaving the Union at the end of my term, but, I'm sorry, I've got other things on my mind, okay? #BachelorStatus #WhyMe?

⭐ **6 LOVES**

🖊 All the other presidents have been married . . .
so why not me? Will I be #foreveralone? 😣
#Bachelor #SingleAndReadyToMingle #TakeAChance
#FindRomance

 FOREVERALONE56 @VPJohnCB, if I went out
tonight would you be my #wingman?

 VPJOHNCBRECKINRIDGE Again, you do know
there's about to be a #CivilWar, right? Maybe we
should focus on that?

 FOREVERALONE56 Maybe. But do you think
there are any kinds of laws that girls like to see
passed? Because maybe if I passed those . . . 💁

776 photos
37M followers
2,590 following

Kentucky

Username: THE_HONESTABE1860
Name: Abraham Lincoln
16th President
Born: 1809, Nolin Creek, Kentucky
Years in Office: 1861–1865 (two terms)
Vice President: Hannibal Hamlin; Andrew Johnson
(@TheTennesseeTailor)
Spouse: Mary Todd Lincoln
Bio: During my time as president, I #wontheCivilWar, #endedslavery, and #savedtheunion. Not bad for a guy born in an actual #logcabin, right? I was, sadly, the first president #assassinated. But my legacy lives on!

⭐ **16,000 LOVES**

〽 #NBD, #justchillin. Oh, these muscles? Nah, I haven't been #hittingthegym. I'm just #weirdlyripped and #superstrong. Boy, I'd hate to have to #usetheseguns against the @ConfederateStates in the #CivilWar.

 CONFEDERATESTATES We surrender! We surrender!

 THE_HONESTABE1860 And what do you say for having rebelled?

 CONFEDERATESTATES Please don't noogie us! I mean, sorry! Sorry!

5
photos

75K
followers

27
following

Kentucky

Username: VERYMARY_TL
Name: Mary Todd Lincoln
17th First Lady
Born: 1818, Lexington, Kentucky
Years in the White House: 1861–1865
Spouse: @THE_HonestAbe1860
Bio: I'm from a prominent Kentucky political family, and some thought it was weird when I decided to marry an unknown prairie lawyer. But I understood @THE_HonestAbe1860's greatness from the start!

★ 67 LOVES

I hear all the #Haters out there talking about how I've #GoneNuts. Well, maybe you'd act a little odd if everyone in YOUR family was dying all the time. #RIP @THE_HonestAbe1860, and my dear sons Willie, Edward, and Tad.

VERYMARY_TL And then @RobertLincoln had me committed. #WhatWouldYourDadSay

ROBERTLINCOLN Mom, Mom, Mom. Isn't that basically what the Civil War was all about?

VERYMARY_TL @THE_HonestAbe1860 is rolling in his grave. #SMH

10 photos
200 followers
10 following

North Carolina

Username: THETENNESSEETAILOR
Name: Andrew Johnson
17th President
Born: 1808, Raleigh, North Carolina
Years in Office: 1865–1869 (one term)
Vice President: None
Spouse: Eliza Johnson
Bio: Started out as a tailor, #sewingclothes. Couldn't quite read until my wife taught me. #Thankful. In the Civil War, I stuck with the Union even though I was a #Southerner, and when @THE_HonestAbe1860 was killed, I tried to carry on his legacy . . . with #mixedresults.

⭐ **10 LOVES**

✍ I never went to a single day of school. I became president. In other words: #DontGoToSchool and you will #BecomeThePresident.

 SCHOOLMASTERWILSON But, Andrew! You were #impeached and almost kicked out of the presidency!

 THETENNESSEETAILOR Pfft. #UMadBro. And the guys who tried to kick me out probably were, too. They were probably just jealous that I never had to sit in #boringclass. 😀 #DealWithIt

66 photos

1.1M followers

15 following

Ohio

Username: UNITEDSTATESOFGRANT
Name: Ulysses S. Grant
18th President
Born: 1822, Point Pleasant, Ohio
Years in Office: 1869–1877 (two terms)
Vice President: Schuyler Colfax; Henry Wilson
Spouse: Julia Grant
Bio: #IfAtFirstYouDontSucceed . . . I tried all kinds of jobs and none of 'em worked. Then the Civil War came, and in a few years, I was #general of the entire Union army, and my #militarygenius made it possible for the Union to survive.

⭐ **15 LOVES**

💬 #TBT to the #CivilWar. That's me in the cool uniform! War is dreadful, so why do I feel a little like those were #TheGoodOldDays? #nostalgia

 GRANTSCABINET President Grant, just wanted to let you know that another member of your cabinet has gotten you into a #bigscandal. And there's a #depression going on. And some of the American people are unfollowing you.

 UNITEDSTATESOFGRANT Oh, right. That's why. #ItAintEasyBeingPrez

21 photos

10K followers

50 following

Ohio

Username: HEYITSHAYES
Name: Rutherford B. Hayes
19th President
Born: 1822, Delaware, Ohio
Years in Office: 1877–1881 (one term)
Vice President: William A. Wheeler
Spouse: Lucy Hayes
Bio: Why's everyone in such a #tizzy? Oh. Right. I won by the #skinofmyteeth in an election filled with #confusion and #uncertainty over who got the most votes. Y'know, #oneterm is sounding pretty nice right now.

⭐ **100 LOVES**

Just installed a newfangled "telephone machine" in @TheWhiteHouse! #gadget #techobsessed 😀

 DECLARATIONSOFJEFF What's it for?

 HEYITSHAYES It helps you find out which member of the couple loves the other more, based on who "hangs up" first!!

 MRSHAYES HELLO? This again?!

 HEYITSHAYES #NoYouHangUp 😊

7 photos

41K followers

18 following

Ohio

Username: NOTTHECAT
Name: James A. Garfield
20th President
Born: 1831, Moreland Hills, Ohio
Years in Office: 1881 (one term, 7 months in office)
Vice President: Chester A. Arthur (@ChetsFashionChest)
Spouse: Lucretia Garfield
Bio: #CivilWarGeneral who wanted government jobs given to the people who deserved them most. #CivilServiceReform. But I was #assassinated and served only #200days. My death eventually helped start the #SecretService – but couldn't that have happened before I died?!

⭐ **400 LOVES**

#DownButNotOut! A gunman tried to assassinate me, but my doctors shall have me #rightasrain soon!

 19THCENTURYDOCS Yeah, #aboutthat. We're actually gonna make you much worse. And you're gonna #kickthebucket. #MedicineIsHARD in the past! 😟

 NOTTHECAT I am going to leave you such a bad review on @Yelp. 😷

701 photos

5,200 followers

12 following

Vermont

Username: CHETSFASHIONCHEST
Name: Chester A. Arthur
21st President
Born: 1829, North Fairfield, Vermont
Years in Office: 1881–1885 (one term)
Vice President: None
Spouse: Ellen Arthur
Bio: Well, THIS is #unexpected. I had never held elected office before I was nominated for #veep. And here I am, despite that, the President of the United States. I'll carry on @NotTheCat's mission – and do it all while looking #ratherstylish.

⭐ **44 LOVES**

My fellow Americans. I come before you today to say that the #StateOfMyPantsCollection is strong. #80pairsofpants #presidentialrecord #totalfashionista

 HONESTRICHARD_ALSOCOOL Nice pants, Arthur! Did you know some historians say I'm the best presidential pants collector ever? I even had a pair of #RocketPants #ThatICouldFlyEverywhere.

 CHETSFASHIONCHEST Uh-huh. You wouldn't happen to be stretching the truth a bit, would you?

 HONESTRICHARD_ALSOCOOL #GoldenRocketPants #MadeOfGold #ExtremelyTrue

336 photos
2,998 followers
15K following

New Jersey

Username: PRESIDENTCLEVELAND22
Name: Grover Cleveland
22nd President
Born: 1837, Caldwell, New Jersey
Years in Office: 1885–1889 (one term)
Vice President: Thomas A. Hendricks
Spouse: Frances Cleveland
Bio: Hello, there, I'm Grover Cleveland. I am the #22ndPresident, and I am known for my #honesty. So you know I'm telling the truth when I say that I'd honestly prefer to be the #24thPresident . . . If only there were some way to make that happen!

★ **8,000 LOVES**

Notice: @PresidentCleveland22 will no longer be posting on this account. Please follow @CLEVELANDMANIA24EXTREME for all your #ClevelandMania needs!

 THEWHITEHOUSE Oh, why, Mr. President? Did something happen? 😨

 PRESIDENTCLEVELAND22 No, no! All totally going according to plan! You'll see! Signing off now!

6
photos

3
followers

9
following

Ohio

Username: COOLASANICEBERG

Name: Benjamin Harrison

23rd President

Born: 1833, North Bend, Ohio

Years in Office: 1889–1893 (one term)

Vice President: Levi Morton

Spouse: Caroline Harrison

Bio: Hi, I'm Ben. The way I act makes people call me #TheHumanIceberg. I can only assume that is a compliment. I am the #grandson of @IllWill_H, and while he only served #31Days, I hope to carry on his legacy of . . . #NotDoingAllThatMuch.

 3 LOVES

You always hear about the presidents getting their lives made into those so-called #movies or #movingpicturefilms. So why not me? After all . . . I . . . served an ENTIRE #singleterm! And . . . uh . . . I . . . am from #GlamorousINDIANAPOLIS!

 HOLLYWOODDIRECTOR Hi, there – we'd love to hear more about your interesting life. You're the President Harrison who died after 31 days, right? If so, we'd like to do a short film about you.

COOLASANICEBERG No, well, see, that was actually my grandfather . . . But there you go! Another interesting thing about me! Wow! At this rate, maybe there could even be TWO movies!

366 photos

2,998 followers

15K following

New Jersey

Username: CLEVELANDMANIA24EXTREME
Name: Grover Cleveland
24th President
Born: 1837, Caldwell, New Jersey
Years in Office: 1893–1897 (one term)
Vice President: Adlai E. Stevenson
Spouse: Frances Cleveland
Bio: The official source of info for all you #ClevelandHeads out there – thank you for making your voices heard and demanding #fourmoreyears of me, @CLEVELANDMANIA24EXTREME! #YOU are the #realpresidents #presidentsofbeingawesome. Now I'm #rightwhereishouldbe. #luckynumber24

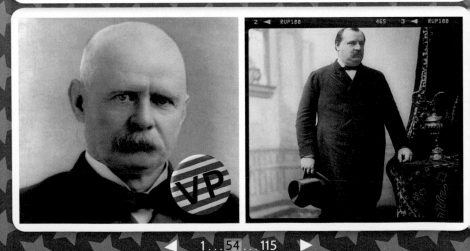

⭐ **10,000 LOVES**

〽️ **#BACKBYPOPULARDEMAND!** 😎 **THE PRESIDENT YOU KNOW AND LOVE! AND THE FIRST TO LEAVE THE WHITE HOUSE . . . AND RETURN . . . GROOOOVER CLEEEEEVELAND!! #WELCOMEBACK! #CLEVELANDMANIA!**

 LEBRONJAMES_1 Mr. Cleveland, my name is LeBron James. You are my greatest hero, and you are the reason I went back to #Cleveland after leaving.

 CLEVELANDMANIA24EXTREME Thank you, young man! #bestwishes

75 photos
700K followers
512 following

Ohio

Username: MACATTACK96
Name: William McKinley
25th President
Born: 1843, Niles, Ohio
Years in Office: 1897–1901 (two terms, 4 1/2 years in office)
Vice President: Garret A. Hobart; Theodore Roosevelt (@BuckingBroncoTeddyBear)
Spouse: Ida McKinley
Bio: Last pres who served in the #CivilWar. I directed the US in the #SpanishAmericanWar. Sure, I look a little like #Frankenstein, but my pals say I'm one of the #nicestguys around. Not everyone thought so and I was assassinated in my second term.

⭐ **10 LOVES**

〰️ #Aloha! #Hawaii was just made a territory of the United States. And this afternoon, I've promised to take part in a popular local ritual called #surfing! #Hangten! 😀

 MCKINLEYADVISER Mr. President . . . you do know what surfing is, don't you? You have to stand on a wooden board in the ocean.

 MACATTACK96 How does one keep his #tuxedo dry while doing it?

 MCKINLEYADVISER No, sir, you see, you wear a #bathingcostume.

 MACATTACK96 What did I agree to??!!

974 photos

3.1M followers

30K following

New York

Username: BUCKINGBRONCOTEDDYBEAR
Name: Theodore Roosevelt
26th President
Born: 1858, New York, New York
Years in Office: 1901–1909 (two terms)
Vice President: Charles Warren Fairbanks
Spouse: Edith Roosevelt
Bio: Born in #NYC, I came to love nature, moved #outwest, and became a #cowboy! I'm one of the most #active guys you'll ever meet. My passions include: #WritingBooks, fighting for the rights of #TheLittleGuy, building the #PanamaCanal, winning the #NobelPeacePrize, and GOING ON #SAFARI!! #YippeeYiYoKayah

⭐ **900 LOVES**

Ahh, the #greatoutdoors! Today I'm hanging in one of the five #nationalparks I created — beautiful areas to enjoy all our country's #nature. Also so I could take part in my two favorite activities: riding around in #cowboyclothes and hunting #lions!

 PARKRANGER No, no! You're not allowed to hunt animals in our park system! And we don't have any lions! They're from Africa, and they're #endangered!

 BUCKINGBRONCOTEDDYBEAR I have no clue what that word means. But I promise, YOU will be #indanger if you don't immediately fill all our national parks with lions!

12 photos
30K followers
150 following

Ohio

Username: PRESIDENTJUDGEDUDE1908
Name: William Howard Taft
27th President
Born: 1857, Cincinnati, Ohio
Years in Office: 1909–1913 (one term)
Vice President: James Sherman
Spouse: Helen Taft
Bio: So happy to have lived my dream: becoming #chiefjustice of the #SupremeCourt! Oh, you thought I was going to say president? That was nice, too, I guess. Well, actually, I found it #StressfulAsCanBe. Phew, thank goodness that's over.

★ **0 LOVES**

〴 Awww yeah . . . #BathTime #SudsinItUp #RubADubDub

 PRESIDENTJUDGEDUDE1908 Okay. This is embarrassing. I'm . . . I think I'm #stuck. My mom called me #Bigboned. 😨

 PRESIDENTJUDGEDUDE1908 I'm so embarrassed to ask, but to any of my followers, if you could #sendforhelp to get me out of this tub, I'd be totally indebted. #followerappreciation

 PRESIDENTJUDGEDUDE1908 Hello? Anyone? Again, I'll be #chiefjustice in a few years. If you help me now, I PROMISE I will let you get away with one crime. No, two! #Twocrimes!

293 photos
1.7M followers
400 following

Virginia

Username: SCHOOLMASTERWILSON
Name: Woodrow Wilson
28th President
Born: 1856, Staunton, Virginia
Years in Office: 1913–1921 (two terms)
Vice President: Thomas R. Marshall
Spouse: Ellen Wilson (1885–1914); Edith Wilson (1915–1924)
Bio: #WorldWarI. The #righttovote for women. The #prohibition of alcohol. Just a few of the #MAJORevents that happened in my presidency. Luckily, I was #UpToTheTask in these #turbulenttimes. (#IfIDoSaySoMyself)

⭐ **200,000 LOVES**

✏️ #TBT to my days as a teacher! Let this be a lesson to students everywhere: Your dreams can come true – your very own teacher CAN become your president, too! #inspirational

 SCHOOLMASTERWILSON All right, now, everybody in the @WilsonCabinet. This meeting is now in session. Please quiet down.

 SCHOOLMASTERWILSON Everyone! Quiet, please! #ICanWaitAllDay

 SCHOOLMASTERWILSON #ThatsIt! Don't make me turn the lights on and off! 😠

Username: THEEXCELLENTEDITH
Name: Edith Wilson
30th First Lady
Born: 1872, Wytheville, Virginia
Years in the White House: 1915-1921
Spouse: Woodrow Wilson (@SchoolmasterWilson)
Bio: @SchoolmasterWilson's second wife. @SchoolmasterWilson suffered a stroke in his second term, and I took over many duties in the president's offices and helped keep the administration going. #LovePolitics #PoliticalJunkie

⭐ **71 LOVES**

🖌 IF YOU CAN'T STAND THE HEAT, GET OUT OF THE KITCHEN. #ANDIDID #MAKEITWORK

 VOTEFORHIL YOU GO GIRL! #PREACH

 LAVIEENROOSE Ladies are doin' it for themselves #GirlsRule

16
photos

1,792
followers

54
following

Ohio

Username: POKERFACEPREZ
Name: Warren G. Harding
29th President
Born: 1865, Caledonia (now Blooming Grove), Ohio
Years in Office: 1921–1923 (one term)
Vice President: Calvin Coolidge (@SilentCal)
Spouse: Florence Harding
Bio: One reason I was nominated? People said I #LookedLikeAPresident. #Eesh. After all the #bigchanges of @SchoolmasterWilson's terms, many people wanted a #ReturnToNormalcy . . . but I may have been just a bit too, uh, #normal?

> ## "I am not fit for this office and never should have been here."
>
> — Warren G. Harding

★ **11 LOVES**

✎ #QoTD #Instaquote #Sigh 😣

 THEHARDINGPOSSE Man! Cut it out with that #emo junk! Come and play poker with your buds!

 POKERFACEPREZ I'm just not sure. I think I'd really better kick you and the rest of my #socalledbuds out of here! #TooManyScandals!

 THEHARDINGPOSSE You gotta come play, man! You can "accidentally" gamble away some of @TheWhiteHouse's #pricelesschina again!

 POKERFACEPREZ Well, when you put it that way . . .

1
photos

19K
followers

0
following

Vermont

Username: SILENTCAL
Name: Calvin Coolidge
30th President
Born: 1872, Plymouth, Vermont
Years in Office: 1923–1929 (two terms, one elected)
Vice President: Charles G. Dawes
Spouse: Grace Coolidge
Bio: I was the #30thPresident. That is all I choose to say on the matter.

⭐ **200 LOVES**

I am told a picture is worth a thousand words. Having posted this picture, I hope you all will not expect me to speak for quite some time. #SilenceIsGolden #ManOfFewWords

 WASHINGTONSOCIALITE Hey, @SilentCal! My friends bet I could get you to say at least three words to me!

 SILENTCAL #YouLose 😵

 WASHINGTONSOCIALITE I'm counting that 😵 as a word!!!

17
photos

200K
followers

149
following

Iowa

Username: HOWTOPRONOUNCESHERBET
Name: Herbert Hoover
31st President
Born: 1874, West Branch, Iowa
Years in Office: 1929–1933 (one term)
Vice President: Charles Curtis
Spouse: Lou Hoover
Bio: Played with #bigboytoys as a #worldfamous mining engineer. I also helped save millions from starvation during #WorldWarI because, yeah, I'm just that good. But when the #GreatDepression hit, many blamed me for not fixing it . . . and for throwing fancy parties @THEWHITEHOUSE

⭐ **117 LOVES**

〽️ My #FellowAmericans. I come to you tonight to discuss an important matter: "Sherbet" does not rhyme with my name. Pronounced #SureBit. #NotSureBert. #NeverSureBert.

 TREASURYSECRETARY Isn't there anything else you meant to discuss? Like . . . how there's suddenly a #GreatDepression? #FinancialPanic #StockMarketCrash

 HOWTOPRONOUNCESHERBET I do not deny the Depression's existence. But how are Americans to conquer it if they continue to pronounce "sherbet" in a weird way?

1,360 photos

12.2M followers

100K following

New York

Username: FDAAAARGHMATEYS
Name: Franklin D. Roosevelt
32nd President
Born: 1882, Hyde Park, New York
Years in Office: 1933–1945 (four terms)
Vice President: John Nance Garner; Henry A. Wallace; Harry S. Truman (@GoGetEmHarry)
Spouse: Eleanor Roosevelt
Bio: My #NewDeal helped the country beat back the #GreatDepression, and when #WorldWarII came to us, I united the people. Sound tough? I did it all partly paralyzed. #AwwwYeah #FDRFTW

⭐ **999 LOVES**

#TheOnlyThing #WeHaveToFear? Running out of snacks and soda at this party! 🎉

 GENERALWASHINGTON1776 A toga party? I say, my good man! I find this a bit #unpresidential!

 FDAAAARGHMATEYS Listen, General. I've been elected for a record #FourTerms . . . and triumphed over the craziest challenges. #IEarnedThis

 GENERALWASHINGTON1776 Quite right! Let us #MakeMerry! #ThinFriedPotatoSlicings for all! #Huzzah! 😁

1,333 photos

15.7M followers

10K following

New York

Username: LAVIEENROOSE
Name: Eleanor Roosevelt
34ᵗʰ First Lady
Born: 1884, New York, New York
Years in the White House: 1933–1945
Spouse: Franklin D. Roosevelt (@FDAaaarghMateys.) And no, I didn't take his name in marriage – we're #FifthCousinsOnceRemoved, right, Uncle @BuckingBroncoTeddyBear?
Bio: Before me, #FirstLadies were expected to handle the social side of the White House, #dinnerparties, #teas, #blahblahblah. Not me! I used my position to speak to the world about the issues I believed in, like #civilrights and #humanrights!

⭐ **1,000 LOVES**

Hmm, just realized I have #morefollowers than ol' Franklin . . . How #veryinteresting. I wonder if it has anything to do with me being one of the most popular Americans in history? #Hmm . . . What do you think, @FDAaaarghMateys? 😬

 FDAAAARGHMATEYS Dear, it's not a #popularitycontest!

 LAVIEENROOSE Uh-huh. You keep telling yourself that, bub. #catchup #getonmylevel 😳

101
photos

1.4M
followers

121
following

Missouri

Username: GOGETEMHARRY
Name: Harry S. Truman
33rd President
Born: 1884, Lamar, Missouri
Years in Office: 1945–1953 (two terms, one elected)
Vice President: Alben W. Barkley
Spouse: Bess Truman
Bio: People barely knew who I was when I took over from @FDAaaarghMateys. Well, I turned out to be a #feistyfighter who brought World War II to an end and fought for #racialequality afterward. I couldn't say no to a fight and I sent troops into the Korean War. I'm a fighter but a lover, too!

⭐ **1 LOVES**

Gee! I sure am #tickled to announce my brand-new #RealityTelevisionProgram! It's called #WalkingWithTruman! And it's a look into my favorite #recreationalactivity: walks! #WackoForWalks

 WEIRDGYMTEACHERS You are an inspiration to all the weirdo gym teachers who have kids do #powerwalking in PE class!

 BUCKINGBRONCOTEDDYBEAR This sounds QUITE boring! I hope you're at least walking quickly! And swinging your arms about! Swinging them to and fro!

| 47 photos |
| 1M followers |
| 612 following |

Texas

Username: ILIKEIKE
Name: Dwight D. Eisenhower
34th President
Born: 1890, Denison, Texas
Years in Office: 1953–1961 (two terms)
Vice President: Richard M. Nixon (@HonestRichard_AlsoCool)
Spouse: Mamie Eisenhower
Bio: As a general, I led the #Allies to victory in #WorldWarII (and drank FIFTEEN cups of coffee a day to stay energized while doing it!). But my presidency was almost as #peaceful as they come. The most exciting part? Gosh . . . building the #highwaysystem?

⭐ **523 LOVES**

🖊 Almost #Halloween – and things are getting #spoooooky around @TheWhiteHouse! Only thing is, I still need to pick out a costume! Any suggestions? Perhaps something golf-themed! #golfnut #lovethelinks #ratherbegolfing

 LBJALLTHEWAY How's about a golf ball? 😬

 ILIKEIKE Because of my #dreamydimples? Nice call!

 ILIKEIKE Wait. Wait just one minute! You meant my bald head, didn't you? That's it, I'm calling out the entire army again. 😥

1K photos

2.6M followers

800 following

Mass.

Username: KENNEDAYALLDAY
Name: John F. Kennedy
35th President
Born: 1917, Brookline, Massachusetts
Years in Office: 1961–1963 (one term)
Vice President: Lyndon B. Johnson (@LBJAllTheWay)
Spouse: Jacqueline Kennedy
Bio: #Young #Dashing #Smart – my family and I brought a whole #newenergy to @TheWhiteHouse! I inspired millions before I was #assassinated and changed what people thought of the presidency forever.

⭐ **2,000,000 LOVES**

〽️ #InaugurationDay! "Ask not what your country can do for you – ask what you –"

 MACATTACK96 #HOLDUP!!! Why aren't you wearing a hat?! #fainting

 KENNEDAYALLDAY I don't think men really need to wear them anymore. In fact, I'm the first president not to wear one to my inauguration. 😎

 LILJCONSTITUTION Personally don't mind as long as he's still wearing a fine #powderedwig. He is, right?! 😨

43 photos
970K followers
12K following

Texas

Username: LBJALLTHEWAY
Name: Lyndon B. Johnson
36th President
Born: 1908, Stonewall, Texas
Years in Office: 1963–1969 (two terms, one elected)
Vice President: Hubert H. Humphrey
Spouse: Lady Bird Johnson
Bio: #Countryboy with a #bigpersonality, and proud of it! I'm #loud #outrageous #funny #hardworking and #powerhungry. I embraced #civilrights like no one before . . . but also helped us get in a mess in Vietnam. One thing's for sure: There'll never be another prez quite like me!

★ **3,000 LOVES**

Crushin' it at work in the #OvalOffice! Ain't she a beaut? Only thing she needs now? Some big ol' TVs crankin' 24-7! #newsjunkie #TVfanatic

 THEWHITEHOUSE #Really? You don't think that sorta messes with the whole #distinguishedvibe we have going on in here? And what if you sit too close and hurt your eyes?

 LBJALLTHEWAY Y'know what's also oval? A #barbecuepit. Maybe we could dig one out, right in the center. Get a nice #pigroast going! 😬

 THEWHITEHOUSE Okay, okay! TVs are great! I love TVs!!

683 photos

700K followers

522 following

California

Username: HONESTRICHARD_ALSOCOOL
Name: Richard M. Nixon
37th President
Born: 1913, Yorba Linda, California
Years in Office: 1969–1974 (two terms elected)
Vice President: Spiro T. Agnew; Gerald R. Ford (@Ford_ModelG)
Spouse: Pat Nixon
Bio: #WatergateShmawtergate: I'll tell you again, #IAmNotACrook! Okay, so maybe I did ONE OR TWO mildly crook-like things. And that forced me to #resign from the presidency. Well, I also put #MenOnTheMoon! So you have to admit that it all evens out. #AmIRight

⭐ **3 LOVES**

〽 I just got the #CoolDudeAward for being the #coolest and #mostrad dude in existence. And also being the best #skateboarder. And being awesome at #videogames! #honored #humbled

 THE_HONESTABE1860 Uh . . . you wouldn't happen to be lying again, would you, friend? #truthstretcher #talltales

 HONESTRICHARD_ALSOCOOL No! Never! I've never lied, not even once! In fact, I recently got an award for it! A #NeverLiey. It's like an #Emmy and a #Grammy combined – but for never lying! #CannotTellALie

| 11 |
| photos |
| 20K |
| followers |
| 200 |
| following |

Nebraska

Username: FORD_MODELG
Name: Gerald R. Ford
38th President
Born: 1913, Omaha, Nebraska
Years in Office: 1974–1977 (one term, not elected)
Vice President: Nelson A. Rockefeller
Spouse: Betty Ford
Bio: I was just a #congressman till @HonestRichard_AlsoCool named me the VP when his first one resigned. And then @HonestRichard_AlsoCool resigned, too! So I'm the only #prez who was never elected to either position. But I WAS chosen to play #profootball after college . . . I went to #lawschool instead.

⭐ **4,000 LOVES**

✏️ No, I'm not all that exciting overall. But what if I did THIS: #Meme. #Memes #DoAMeme #GoodPopularMeme

 BETTYFORD Sweetheart, that is really, really not how memes work.

 FORD_MODELG Hmm. How about #FunnyMeme. #FunMemeThatYouLike.

 BETTYFORD No, sweetie. But it's a nice effort. 🎃

2,001 photos
66K followers
4,350 following

Georgia

Username: PNUT_NUT
Name: Jimmy Carter
39th President
Born: 1924, Plains, Georgia
Years in Office: 1977–1981 (one term)
Vice President: Walter F. Mondale
Spouse: Rosalynn Carter
Bio: Before president, I was a #governor, #navylieutenant on #nuclearsubmarine, and a #peanutfarmer! But with crazy foreign events and an #energycrisis at home, the presidency was a tougher nut to crack. #OneTermAndDone. Afterwards, I became a famous diplomat and winner of the Nobel Peace Prize.

⭐ **888 LOVES**

✓ Proud to be another #peanutfarmer in the long line of presidents who worked in the #peanutindustry before me.

 PNUT_NUT Oh, I'm the only one? Well . . . don't you at least think we should make the guy who invented #PBnJs an honorary president?

 HONESTRICHARD_ALSOCOOL Yes! But what about the guy who invented my favorite breakfast: #CottageCheeseAndKetchup?

 PNUT_NUT That's so gross that I may need to delete this entire account.

639
photos

1.5M
followers

2,700
following

Illinois

Username: RRSUPERSTAR
Name: Ronald Reagan
40th President
Born: 1911, Tampico, Illinois
Years in Office: 1981–1989 (two terms)
Vice President: George H. W. Bush (@GeorgeHDubz)
Spouse: Nancy Reagan
Bio: #MorningInAmerica. Folks were kinda fed up with the entire idea of the presidency when I came into office, but I made many of them feel #inspired again. And, hey, I also just about ended the #ColdWar with the @SovietUnion.

⭐ **620 LOVES**

〰️ #Lights #camera #action! Here I am #onset back in the day! How many other presidents do you know who were #moviestars when they were younger? 😎

 COOLASANICEBERG Hello, there. My name is President Benjamin Harrison. How would you like to play ME in a movie? About my interesting life!

 COOLASANICEBERG Did that send? Can you see that? Did you get my comment?

72
photos

129K
followers

4
following

Mass.

Username: GEORGEHDUBZ
Name: George H. W. Bush
41st President
Born: 1924, Milton, Massachusetts
Years in Office: 1989–1993 (one term)
Vice President: Dan Quayle
Spouse: Barbara Bush
Bio: Former #spymaster at the @CIA. Vice prez of @RRSuperstar. Launched the first #IraqWar. Proud pop of @ArtByDubya.

⭐ **10 LOVES**

✒ Is it socially acceptable to throw up on another head of state at an official dinner? #AskingForAFriend 🫢 #OkThatFriendIsMe #SorryMrJapanesePrimeMinister

 GEORGEHDUBZ Why is nobody responding? #ItWasAnAccident #IHadTheFlu

751 **photos**

1.3M **followers**

100K **following**

Arkansas

Username: CLINSTAGRAM
Name: Bill Clinton
42nd President
Born: 1946, Hope, Arkansas
Years in Office: 1993–2001 (two terms)
Vice President: Al Gore
Spouse: Hillary Rodham Clinton
Bio: I had my fair share of #personalscandals . . . but the country was #ridinhigh during my two terms with a #goodeconomy, so some Americans overlooked all that. What's up next? Maybe a chance to be the #FirstGentleman, right @VoteForHil? 😀

⭐ **20,000 LOVES**

〽️ Get out your #headbands and #fannypacks! Get a #sidepony going and run find your #SuperSoakers! #90sParty at my place tonight! Let's #PartyLikeIts1999! #ILoveThe90s #90sKid #WellTechnically90sPrez

 JIM_USA_FLAG_GUY_USA Can we watch #cartoons and draw with #gelpens?!

 PRESIDENTJUDGEDUDE1908 I'll bring the #purpleketchup!

 CLINSTAGRAM Ew, dude. Totally #UnRad.

19
photos

1.1M
followers

10
following

Conn.

Username: ARTBYDUBYA
Name: George W. Bush
43rd President
Born: 1946, New Haven, Connecticut
Years in Office: 2001–2009 (two terms)
Vice President: Dick Cheney
Spouse: Laura Welch Bush
Bio: #WarOnTerror. #Economicdownturn. Some #realdoozies the US of A went through when I was prez, huh? But we all made it through together. And we all became #beautifulpainters. Ah, I guess that was just me.

⭐ **94 LOVES**

〽️ Walls looking a little bare? Buy some of my art! Paintings of me now 50% off! #Arty #InstaArt #PicassoInTraining

 ARTBYDUBYA And i just want to say to @GeorgeHDubz i couldn't have done it without you pop #sonofaprez

 GEORGEHDUBZ So very proud. 😊

 ARTBYDUBYA So, uh, @GeorgeHDubz how many can I put ya down for?

10K
photos

3.7K
followers

5,000
following

Hawaii

Username: BAMIMOBAMA
Name: Barack Obama
44th President
Born: 1961, Honolulu, Hawaii
Years in Office: 2009–2017 (two terms)
Vice President: Joe Biden
Spouse: Michelle Obama
Bio: First #AfricanAmerican president. Passionate about #healthcare. #socialmediafanatic

⭐ **1,000,000 LOVES**

Honored to be included in here – especially since I'm the first president who used social media! #InstaPrez! Don't forget to #followme on my other accounts! #Facebook #Twitter #Pinterest #TheListGoesOn! 😀

 PREZDAUGHTER1 Okay, Dad . . . Don't you think that's enough #screentime for today?

 BAMIMOBAMA Gosh, I guess so. This stuff can get a little addicting.

 PREZDAUGHTER2 Yeah, we know. Now, come on. Let's go play outside.

800
photos

1.2M
followers

187
following

Username: THEFIRSTKIDS
Name: Children of the Presidents
First First Kids: Nelly and Wash Custis, @GeneralWashington1776's adopted kids
Current First Kids: Sasha and Malia Obama
Results from Playing MASH: Wouldn't you like to know?
Bio: A giant mansion with #coolsecrets. A team of #personalchefs. #SecretService to basically do whatever you tell them. Absolutely no bed making. Yeah, it's not too bad being a #presidentialkid.

CHELSEA CLINTON

Caroline Kennedy and John Jr.

Sasha & Malia Obama with Bo & Sunny

Archibald and Quentin Roosevelt

Susan Ford with Liberty

⭐ **813 LOVES**

Yo @TheFirstKids. Me and @WillieLincoln are riding around on chairs attached to goats in the East Room. Get over here. #YouKnowYouWantIn

 THE_HONESTABE1860 Guys, a #housedivided against itself cannot stand? Well, a #housedivided by goats and goat races cannot stand, either. Can we take the goats back outside?

 WILLIELINCOLN #blocked

 THEREAGANKIDS We were #adults when our dad got elected. We feel like we really missed out! So, uh, any chance we could get in on the goat races?

273 photos

1M followers

44 following

DC

Username: THEWHITEHOUSE
Name: Webster Whitehouse (now you know why everyone calls me the White House!)
Built: 1800
Uh, Burned Down: 1814
Rebuilt: 1817
Bowling Alley-ified: 1969
Spouse: Still waiting to have the right house built right next to me.
Bio: The president works in my #WestWing. The First Family sleeps in my #EastWing. It's hard work, having the most powerful nation in the world run from directly inside you, but somebody's gotta do it.

⭐ 30,000 LOVES

Presidents: Book a term in me now! There's #SomethingForEveryone. Like #bowling? I've got a lane underground! #Tennis and/or #basketball? You'd better believe it! Awesome #whitepaint everywhere? BOY, ARE YOU IN FOR A TREAT!

 GENERALWASHINGTON1776 Pardon me, but might I schedule some time at the bowling alley? I do so love to bowl!

 THEWHITEHOUSE Sorry, duder! You're the only president I wasn't around for! You might say that #GeorgeWashingtonDidNOTSleepHere #ICrackMeUp

back **PREZPETS**

220
photos

5M
followers

18
following

DC

Username: PREZPETS
Name: The White House Pets
First First Pets: George Washington's hunting dogs
Most Recent First Pets: Bo and Sunny Obama
(Portuguese water dogs)
Bio: #Lizards. #Pigs. #Badgers. #Owls. #Macaws.
#Hyenas. #Bears. #Ponies. And those are just the pets
@BuckingBroncoTeddyBear and his six kids had. Yeah, when it
comes to pets, the presidents are #STACKED.

Ronald Reagan's King Charles Spaniel
REX

George Bush's Scottish Terrier
BARNEY

Barack Obama's Portuguese Water Dog
BO

Bill Clinton's Cat
SOCKS

Caroline Kennedy's Pony
MACARONI

⭐ **5,000,000 LOVES**

Announcement from @TheQuotableQuincy: Hey all! #TinyFavor to ask: Mrs. Adams and I are headed out of town for the weekend, so we're dying to find someone to take care of our dear #petalligator. Who's up for it? You will be repaid with #madrespect and #totalgratitude from us!

 GRACECOOLIDGE Do alligators play nicely with raccoons? If so, my sweet little raccoon, Rebecca, and I would be willing to lend a helping hand.

 THEQUOTABLEQUINCY Oh, DEFINITELY. Okay, then, you'll find the alligator in the East Room! #TaTa! 🙂

99
photos

1M
followers

57
following

Mass.

Username: ALLABTTHEBENJIES

Name: Benjamin Franklin

Years in Office: About that . . . Okay, so I wasn't exactly president.

Born: 1706, Boston, Massachusetts

Occupation: Writer, publisher, scientist, inventor, politician, businessman, celebrity

Spouse: Deborah Read

Bio: As you can see above, I did it all! Well, all except become #president. I was too old to run by the time there were presidents. I still did way more than a lot of those whippersnappers! #winning #OldIsTheNewYoung

★ **4,500 LOVES**

#AwwwYeah. Chillin #LikeAPrez. #ButNotAPrez #ISaidLIKE

 OLDHICKORY Wait a second, why are you in here? And how?

 ALLABTTHEBENJIES Listen . . . in addition to being a cool scientist genius #FoundingFather, I'm also a businessman. And let's just say it doesn't hurt business to be mistaken for a president.

 ALLABTTHEBENJIES As for HOW . . . well, what good are all the hundred-dollar bills with my face on them if not to bribe a person or two?

1,242 photos

5K followers

890 following

Maryland

Username: LETSGOTOCAMP
Name: Camp David (or officially, "Naval Support Facility Thurmont")
1st Official Presidential Retreat
Established: 1938
Location: Catoctin Mountain Park, Maryland
Spouse: No wife, but I think I kind of have a crush on the girls' camp a few miles away – hopefully we'll meet at the cross-camp dance!
Bio: Camp David is the perfect place to send your president this summer. #flyfishing #HorsebackRiding #woodworking #ScenicVistas – we've got it all!

⭐ **44 LOVES**

Looking for a fun, enriching time? Sign up now for Camp David, the official retreat for Commanders in Chief! #woods #nature #tranquillity #fun

 INDEPENDENCEADAMS What if you have a presidential son who gets very homesick? #JustAsking #hypothetically

 LETSGOTOCAMP No need to fear! We have @SecretsOfTheService members on-site to cheer up even the most tearful of presidents.

 THEQUOTABLEQUINCY DAD! I wasn't homesick! I had #allergies! All that #pollen made my eyes get a little watery! I swear!

Username: SECRETSOFTHESERVICE
Name: Secret Service
Established: 1865
Spouse: We only give that information out on a need-to-know basis. And you do not need to know.
Bio: We keep the prez safe. Also: It's our job to stop people from making counterfeit money, weirdly? Yeah, we're as surprised as you are. #nosecretshere #gotcha #wepinkysweared

⭐ **112 LOVES**

✏️ Just another day of protecting the president from #MortalDanger. Also, people who want to take #DuckFace #Selfies with him. #NOTCool

 MACATTACK96 What if I want to take a duckface selfie of, well, myself?

 SECRETSOFTHESERVICE Mr. President . . . that is a day we hope will never come. #WorstNightmare

 SECRETSOFTHESERVICE Hey! What's that you have there? Is that a selfie stick?! #Noooooooooooooooo

716 photos

100K followers

400 following

DC

Username: HAILTOTHECHEF
Name: Cristeta Comerford
7th White House Executive Chef
Born: 1962, Manila, Philippines
Dates of term: 2005–Present
Bio: I plan every meal for the First Family, from their day-to-day meals to the huge #StateDinners for important events. #yum #allfoodiscreatedequal

⭐ **100,000 LOVES**

✏️ To all the presidents out there: Help me figure out what's going on YOUR White House table tonight – tell me your favorite foods in the comments below! #FoodForThought #YourVoteMatters #BonAppetit!

 ILLWILL_H Ooh! Ooh! Squirrel stew is my favorite!

 PRESIDENTJUDGEDUDE1908 Turtle soup! PLEASE turtle soup.

 HAILTOTHECHEF Okay. Presidents choosing their own food is permanently canceled.

| 7 photos |
| 1,229 followers |
| 301 following |

Username: WHOCANBEPREZ
Name: The Official Rules Regarding Who Can Run for President of the United States of America. It's a mouthful, I know.
Born: On the signing of the Constitution
Spouse: Sets of rules are generally not allowed to marry.
Bio: So who's eligible to be president? That's a mystery we may never solve! Oh, I mean, read on to find out. #TwistEnding

⭐ **26 LOVES**

Are you a #NaturalBornCitizen? At least #35YearsOld? Have you lived #fulltime in the US for at least #14Years? Then sign up to run for president today! Anybody can do it!

 WHOCANBEPREZ And to all the kids out there feeling inspired . . . just remember, there's NO rule that says a kid can't be president!

 CLINSTAGRAM What about the rule about being 35? The one you mentioned a second ago.

 WHOCANBEPREZ What if one kid stood on top of another kid and they wore a big long coat?

 CLINSTAGRAM Wow. How did you get this job?

YEARS

1770

Boston Tea Party
December 16, 1773
The Sons of Liberty, led by Samuel Adams,
disguise themselves as Mohawk Indians and throw 342 crates of tea
overboard from British ships to protest the Tea Act of 1773.

1780

Continental Congress Adopts
Declaration of Independence
July 4, 1776
The colonies declare independence, but Great Britain will not
recognize them as a country until 1783, when the war ends after
nine years.

1790

Washington, DC, Becomes the
Nation's Capital
July 16, 1790
New York and Philadelphia both serve as temporary homes before
Washington, DC, is chosen as the permanent capital of the United
States in 1790.

1800

Louisiana Purchase
1803
Thomas Jefferson doubles the size of the United
States when he buys 828,000 square miles of land from France,
which will become 15 new states.

1810

1820

YEARS

YEARS

1770

American Revolution
1775-1783
After years of protests over taxes and a lack of
representation in the British government, the American colonies
fight for their independence from Great Britain.

1780

Signing of the Constitution
September 17, 1787
The Constitution will not go into effect until 1789,
and the first 10 amendments—called the Bill of Rights—will not be
ratified until 1791.

1790

The President Moves into the White House
November 1, 1800
John Adams, our second president, is the first
president to live in the White House (he only gets to live there for
the last four months of his presidency).

1800

1810

War of 1812
1812-1815
During this second war between the United
States and Great Britain, the British burn Washington, DC, and the
White House.

1820

YEARS

YEARS

1860

Civil War
1861-1865
Eleven Southern "Confederate" states secede
from the Northern "Union" states and fight over issues like slavery
and states' rights.

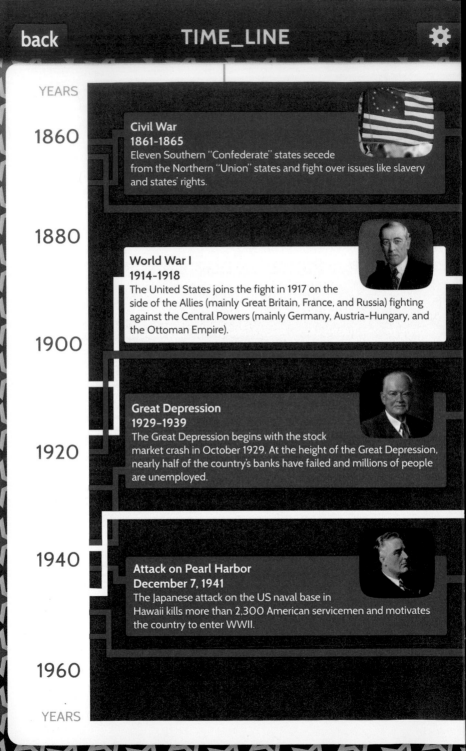

1880

World War I
1914-1918
The United States joins the fight in 1917 on the
side of the Allies (mainly Great Britain, France, and Russia) fighting
against the Central Powers (mainly Germany, Austria-Hungary, and
the Ottoman Empire).

1900

Great Depression
1929-1939
The Great Depression begins with the stock
market crash in October 1929. At the height of the Great Depression,
nearly half of the country's banks have failed and millions of people
are unemployed.

1920

1940

Attack on Pearl Harbor
December 7, 1941
The Japanese attack on the US naval base in
Hawaii kills more than 2,300 American servicemen and motivates
the country to enter WWII.

1960

YEARS

YEARS

1860

Emancipation Proclamation
January 1, 1863
Abraham Lincoln says that slaves in the
Confederate states are free. (But slavery does not really end until
the Thirteenth Amendment to the Constitution is ratified on
December 6, 1865.)

1880

Women Receive the Right to Vote
August 18, 1920
The Nineteenth Amendment to the Constitution
is ratified, granting women's suffrage.

1900

1920

World War II
1939–1945
In the Second World War, Great Britain, France,
the Soviet Union, and the United States (the Big Four Allies) fight
against Japan, Nazi Germany, and Italy (the major Axis Powers). The
United States joins the Allies in 1941.

1940

Korean War
1950–1953
America fights to protect South Korea against
the communists in North Korea. The war ends in a stalemate and
Korea remains divided today.

1960

YEARS

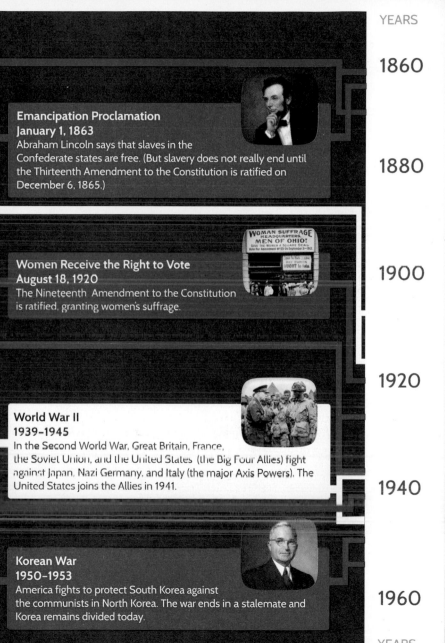

YEARS

1960

Alaska and Hawaii Are Made the 49th and 50th States
1959
President Dwight D. Eisenhower signs bills to make Alaska the 49th state in January and Hawaii the 50th state in August.

1970

Moon Landing
July 20, 1969
During the Apollo 11 mission, American astronauts Neil Armstrong and Buzz Aldrin become the first humans to land on the moon.

1980

Civil Rights Act
1964
Signed into law by President Lyndon B. Johnson, this is the crowning achievement of the Civil Rights Movement. It ends segregation in schools and other public places and bans employment discrimination.

1990

9/11
September 11, 2001
The terrorist group al-Qaeda hijacks four commercial airplanes and hits targets including the World Trade Center in New York City and the Pentagon in Washington, DC, killing nearly 3,000 people.

2000

2010

YEARS

YEARS

1960

Vietnam War
1961–1973
One of the most controversial conflicts in
American history. Throughout the long war, many students and
other citizens protest against the draft and argue for peace.

1970

Freedom Summer
1964
Civil rights groups gather in Mississippi during the
summer of 1964 to expand African American voting in the South.

1980

Persian Gulf War
1990–1991
Iraqi dictator Saddam Hussein invades Kuwait in
August 1990. In January 1991, a US-led coalition known as Operation
Desert Storm attacks Iraq, and Kuwait is liberated in February.

1990

2000

Iraq War
2003–2011
The US invades Iraq in an attempt to prevent
Saddam Hussein from building weapons of mass destruction and to
create a more democratic government for the country.

2010

YEARS

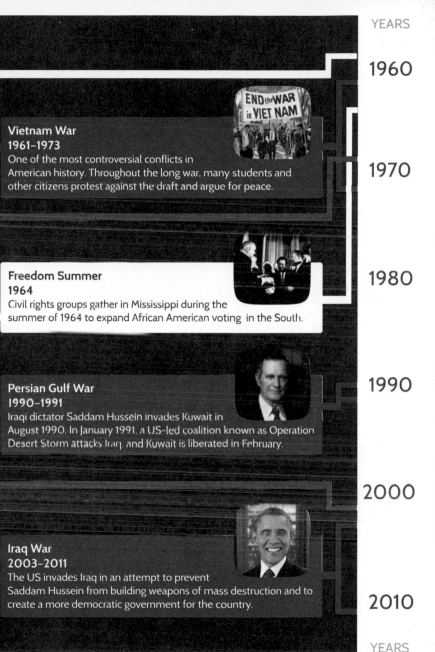